J940·53

D1080302

12/96

SCHOOLS LIBRARY SERVICE
Maltby Library Headquarters
High Street
Maltby
Rotherham S66 8LA

···n 1998

MSC

TOLHURST,
MARILYN

HOME IN THE BLITZ

W & S   56085

£8.50

ROTHERHAM PUBLIC LIBRARIES

This book must be returned by the date specified at the time of
issue as the Date Due for Return.
The loan may be extended (personally, by post or telephone) for
a further period, if the book is not required by another reader,
by quoting the above number   **LM1 (C)**

ROTHERHAM
PUBLIC LIBRARIES
J940.53
741 4636
S6085
SCHOOLS STOCK

WHAT HAPPENED HERE?

HOME IN THE BLITZ

Marilyn Tolhurst
Photographs by Maggie Murray
Illustrations by Gillian Clements

Contents

A & C BLACK · LONDON

What was the Blitz?

The Second World War broke out on Sunday September 3rd 1939. In Britain, the announcement was made on the radio by the Prime Minister, Neville Chamberlain. War had been looming for some time and plans had already been made to protect the population from dangers such as air raids and poison gas attacks. Air raid shelters and gasmasks were issued to everyone. Most children in the cities were moved to safer places in the countryside. Everyone waited nervously for the sound of enemy bombers.

In fact, air raids did not begin until the following year. But when they came, the effects were catastrophic. For London the terror began on the night of September 7th 1940 when 300 German planes flew over the city dropping thousands of tonnes of bombs. The Germans gave the name 'Blitzkrieg' (lightning war) to their swift and deadly raids. Night after night the bombers returned. For Londoners this period was known simply as the 'Blitz'.

The children in this book wanted to find out what life was like during the Blitz so they visited Winston Churchill's Britain at War Experience in London. The museum is near the River Thames, between London Bridge and Tower Bridge and close to the old railway arches that sheltered many Londoners during the air raids.

This is how the city of London looked from a German bomber.

2

The children started their investigation inside the recreated Underground station. They watched a film which explained some of the main events of the war.

A hand-operated air raid siren. This was sounded to warn people that an air raid was expected. The wailing noise of the siren became familiar to all Londoners in 1940.

In December 1940, London was ablaze. St Paul's Cathedral miraculously escaped the bombs and became a symbol of survival in the Blitz.

How do we know about the Blitz?

There is a huge amount of evidence which helps us to understand the war years.

Objects

Objects such as tin hats, tea urns, gasmasks, clothes, toys and even toilet rolls can help us picture the past. Millions of wartime artefacts have survived. Many are displayed or stored in museums. The children saw all sorts of artefacts which have been displayed to recreate life in the Blitz at the Britain at War Experience.

Sights and sounds

Photographs, films and sound recordings made at the time allow us to see events as they happened and to hear the sounds of war. We can watch an air raid complete with sirens, anti-aircraft fire and exploding bombs. We can watch and listen to wartime leaders such as Winston Churchill and Adolf Hitler.

A national identity card. Everyone had to carry one during the war so that they could prove who they were. It was a precaution designed to make it harder for enemy spies to operate in Britain.

Many people who lived through the Blitz are still alive. The children talked to Blanche Overend who, together with her mother and brother, was blown 15m through the air inside an air raid shelter when a bomb hit the house next door. Miraculously they all lived!

Printed material

Wartime newspapers tell us how events were explained at the time, and reveal a lot about how people felt and what they did each day. Government reports, and posters designed to inform and warn the public, are also important sources of information. Some posters used slogans that are still famous, such as 'Careless talk costs lives', warning that idle chatter might give secrets away to enemy spies, and 'Dig for Victory', telling people to grow their own food.

Many written descriptions of the Blitz have survived. This is part of a school essay by Stanton Marcus, a 10 year-old boy who had a lucky escape.

> Suddenly at 3.59am, the next morning everyone awoke. What awoke us was a bomb that had dropped at the back of the house. We jumped out of bed and lit candles (the electric light did not work), then we were surprised. The table leg, from the table, which was upstairs, had come through the ceiling. The only thing that stopped the whole table from falling on my bed were three struts, put in the week before to strengthen the cellar. A beam had dropped from the ceiling, and instead of falling on my cousin's bed, rested on the electric wire. My biggest adventure since the war started.

◀ Many moving films and photographs were taken during the war. This picture shows the effects of blast damage on a house in the East End of London.

5

Time-lines

The first time-line shows some of the important dates in the Second World War. The second time-line shows us some of the important events in Britain during the war years.

1939 – 1945

1939 Germany invades Poland. Britain and France declare war on Germany.

1940 Germany invades Denmark, Norway, Belgium and Holland. Italy enters the war on the side of Germany. The Battle of Britain between the German and British air forces begins, and reaches its peak in September.

1941 Germany invades Russia. Japan bombs the US fleet at Pearl Harbour, Hawaii. Germany and Italy declare war on the United States. The United States enters the war on the side of Britain and Russia.

Events in Britain

1938 Air raid precautions and evacuation plans are first made. Gasmasks are handed out to everyone.

1939 September 1st, cities are blacked out at night. Evacuation begins.

1939 September 3rd. War declared on Germany. Men aged 18-41 are called up for military service. Anderson air raid shelters are delivered to many homes. Identity cards are handed out. Cinemas and theatres close.

December, many evacuees return to the cities as there are no air raids. Cinemas and theatres re-open. This period is known as the 'Phoney War'.

1940 January, food rationing begins.

May, Winston Churchill replaces Chamberlain as Prime Minister. The Home Guard is formed.

August-September. A German invasion plan begins with air attacks on the Royal Air Force. This is known as the Battle of Britain.

September 7th, German air raids (the Blitz) on London begin and continue for 57 nights.

October - November. The Blitz reaches its peak and other cities also become targets.

1941 Food and petrol supplies run short as German U-boats attack ships coming to Britain in the Battle of the Atlantic.

May 11, last major raid of the London Blitz.

1942 Japan invades Burma and takes Singapore. The German advance into Egypt is stopped by the British at El Alamein.

1943 Russia wins the battle of Stalingrad. British and American forces invade Italy. Italy surrenders.

1944 D-Day landings in Normandy. The British, American and allied soldiers take Paris.

1945 The Russian army enters Berlin. Hitler commits suicide. Germany surrenders. US planes drop Atomic bombs on Hiroshima and Nagasaki in Japan. Japan surrenders.

May - June, clothes rationing begins (66 coupons per person per year). The Utility Scheme is introduced.

July, some men are recalled from the armed forces to work in coal mines. Food queues lengthen. The 'Black Market' thrives.

December, single women aged 20-30 are conscripted for military service.

1942 Many more shortages. Clothes coupons reduced to 48 per person per year.

1943 No unemployment in Britain. 90% of single and 80% of married women aged 18-40 are employed in the forces, industry or the Land Army. Coal, petrol, blankets and food are very scarce.

1944 50% of the population go to the cinema each week. Industrial output reaches a peak.

June, the first V1 flying bombs hit London, followed by V2 rockets in September.

December, Home Guard disbanded.

1945 May 8th, Germany surrenders. This is known as VE Day (Victory in Europe). People celebrate in the streets.

War breaks out

As soon as the war began, London became a hive of activity. Everywhere people set to work putting up air raid shelters, blacking out windows, and filling sandbags to protect buildings from bomb blasts. Shop windows were covered with sticky tape to hold the shattered glass together if a bomb dropped close by. Important buildings were camouflaged. Anti-aircraft guns were set up on high ground, and huge barrage balloons were flown to stop enemy aircraft flying low over cities. Practice air raid drills were held to get people used to running into underground shelters.

The headline that everyone dreaded appeared in the Sunday papers on September 3rd 1939.

Some people were very frightened when they realised what might happen. Mrs Wood, who was 30 at the time, recalled 'I was in the garden eating a beetroot sandwich when the news of the war was announced. I was really scared. I thought the end of the world had come.' Others were very excited at the prospect. One boy who was 10 at the time remembers: '. . . me and Stanley set off on our bikes to look for the war. . .' Somebody said they were desperate for people to fill sandbags at the hospital to protect the windows. So we dashed down there. . .'

The people of London waited with bated breath for the bombs to fall. But in fact, bombing did not begin in earnest until the late summer of 1940.

LEAVE THIS TO US SONNY — <u>YOU</u> OUGHT TO BE OUT OF LONDON

MINISTRY OF HEALTH EVACUATION SCHEME

Children were not forced to leave London during the Blitz but posters like this tried to persuade them to go.

This boy is listening to a wartime radio broadcast. He thought that listening to the radio probably helped to keep people cheerful. The radio kept everyone in touch with events. People could tune into the BBC 24 hours a day and listen to music, news and comedy programmes.

The blackout

The blackout was one of the first steps taken to protect Britain from air raids. From September 1st 1939 to September 17th 1944 no-one was allowed to show any lights after sunset. It was hoped that blacking out towns and cities at night would make it harder for enemy bombers to find targets such as shipyards, railways and factories. During the blackout, there were no street lights and, to begin with, no traffic lights or car headlamps. It was even an offence to light a cigarette in the street.

These children tried out some wartime curtains, made of black material. They found that these 'blackout curtains' cut out all the light. During the war, some people used cardboard instead of material to cover their windows. ▶

Burglars and star-gazers enjoyed the blackout but everyone else hated it. White stripes like these were painted on kerbs and other obstacles to help reduce accidents. At night many people carried something white such as a handkerchief or newspaper, so that they could be seen. ▶

In the first year of the war, blackout rules were strict. Anyone caught showing a light could be fined. Everyone had to remember to switch off the hall lights before opening the front door. Air Raid Precaution (ARP) wardens patrolled the streets looking for chinks of light showing through curtains. 'Put out that light' became a familiar cry.

In the blackout it was difficult to find your own front door, let alone the keyhole! A small torch was useful. Larger torches had to be dimmed with two layers of tissue paper.

UNTIL YOUR EYES
GET USED TO
THE DARKNESS,
TAKE IT EASY

LOOK OUT IN THE BLACKOUT

During the blackout, more people were injured in road accidents than by enemy action. Gradually, some rules were relaxed. Traffic lights reappeared, although each light showed only as a tiny cross of coloured light. Cars were allowed a narrow beam of light through masked headlamps. White stripes were painted on trees, lampposts, kerbs and car bumpers. The children were amazed to discover that in the countryside, even black cows were painted white to identify them in the dark.

There were no street lights in the blackout so there were lots of road accidents. This government poster warned people to take care in the dark.

The shelter

As soon as war was declared, every family with a garden received an air raid shelter. These were called Anderson Shelters after the Home Secretary, Sir John Anderson. Over two million shelters were handed out, most of them free.

The Britain at War Experience has a fully fitted Anderson shelter complete with sound effects. The children were horrified by the sound of exploding bombs. Shelters protected people from blast damage and falling masonry but not from a direct hit.

"Don't dance about on it, Winnie, you might fall through."

Anderson Shelters looked like tunnels made from corrugated iron sheets bolted together. The family dug a trench 1 metre deep, roofed this with the iron sheets and covered the roof with soil. Shelters were damp and uncomfortable but each one could protect six people. Air raids mostly happened at night, so many people put bunk beds in their shelters. The children thought that damp and noise would have made sleeping in a shelter very difficult.

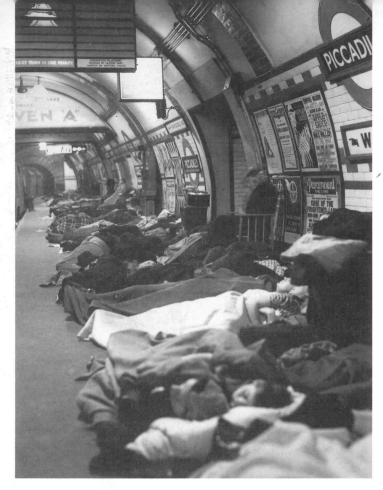

When heavy nighttime air raids began on London, thousands of people sheltered in Underground stations. Here it was warm and dry as well as safe. A white line painted two metres from the edge of the platform marked the area which had to be kept clear so that travellers could get on and off the Underground trains. After 11.30 pm, when the trains stopped running, families armed with sandwiches, rugs and blankets pitched camp for the night on the platforms. Some stations were equipped with bunk beds, toilets and canteens which made nights in the underground a bit more comfortable.

In the winter of 1940, sleeping in the Underground became a way of life for thousands of Londoners. Many families sent a child along in the afternoon to claim a good pitch on the platform. In some stations, concerts entertained the regular guests.

People without gardens were issued with Morrison shelters. These were like metal cages, designed to protect people inside from falling masonry. Many families kept up their spirits by eating biscuits during air raids, but then found themselves sharing their shelter with mice!

Air raid!

The Blitz began on September 7th 1940. First there was the wail of the sirens, then the drone of hundreds of approaching bombers. Finally, came the terrifying noise of exploding bombs. Everyone who could rushed for shelter.

For 57 nights thousands of tonnes of bombs rained down on London. Most of the docks and factories were in the East End, which became the main target of the first attacks. But gradually the rest of the city was hit, including the Houses of Parliament and Buckingham Palace. Over 12,000 people were killed and 20,000 seriously injured.

These children tried rescue work amid the rubble of a bombed out shop at the Britain at War Museum. Realistic sound effects helped give them a vivid idea of how the Blitz really felt. Can you spot the unexploded bomb?

These children examined an incendiary bomb which had been made safe. Wartime children enjoyed collecting bits of shrapnel (metal from bombs) as souvenirs of the Blitz.

During the Blitz, people spent almost every night sleeping in bomb shelters. For those unlucky enough to be 'bombed out', home-life was often very grim. Many people had to crowd in with relatives or move into houses in poor condition. There were mobile bath units and street canteens, but possessions lost in an air raid were almost impossible to replace.

As well as high-explosive bombs, thousands of bombs called incendiaries were dropped. These were designed to start fires. By December 1940 there were 1400 fires raging through the city. London was lit up despite the blackout, and incoming enemy bombers could see their targets perfectly.

An incendiary bomb on the roof could burn down a house within minutes, so everyone kept buckets of sand or earth handy to put out fires. A stirrup pump used with a bucket could be carried anywhere to direct an accurate jet of water on to a fire bomb. The children found the pump very easy to use. Filling up the buckets was much harder work.

Air Raid Precaution (ARP) wardens operated sirens, checked the blackout and organised rescue work after an air raid. The children tried on some ARP uniforms. The wooden rattle was to warn of a gas attack, something which never happened.

15

At home

The children discovered that the war dramatically changed home life for most people. Before 1939, for example, it had been unusual for married women to go out to work. In wartime, almost all women worked. Young children whose fathers were away and whose mothers were out, were looked after at one of the many new day nurseries.

The war brought work for the whole population. Women like these factory workers building tanks, proved they were capable of the heaviest industrial jobs.

Older children learned to take care of themselves. Many fathers were badly missed. 'I put my picture of Daddy up last night and everyone going past had to salute it,' wrote one child.

One of the most popular songs of the war years was called "We'll Meet Again". It reflected the mood of many families who were parted by the war. Here, a soldier says goodbye to his little evacuee son.

The children were amazed to learn that during the war toilet paper was a luxury and was often kept securely locked up! Most people used torn-up pages of the Radio Times for toilet paper.

DIG ON
FOR
VICTORY

Posters like this persuaded people to grow vegetables to make up for food shortages. Most families dug up their lawns to make more room for fruit and vegetables.

Life became a lot less comfortable and convenient. Most basic necessities, such as bread and coal, were in short supply. Petrol shortages kept most private cars off the roads, although buses and taxis continued to run, and bicycles were seen everywhere.

People found it hard to keep clean because no-one was supposed to run a bath more than five inches (12 cm) deep, to save water. There was also a shortage of soap.

Foreign foods, such as chocolate and bananas, were almost impossible to buy, and even ordinary foods were in short supply. In 1940, the Government introduced a way of sharing out the basic necessities more fairly. This was called rationing.

At school

The Blitz completely upset school life. Most schools in the centre of London were moved out of the city, away from the bombing. Many younger teachers left to join the forces. Their places were taken by retired school teachers who worked as long as the war lasted.

The paper shortage meant that there were few school books. Food shortages made school meals more boring than usual. Gasmask practice became part of the school day. Lessons were interrupted whenever there was an air raid alert. Then the whole school trooped down to the air raid shelter to sing songs or recite maths tables. The children met one man at the musuem who recalled sitting in an air raid shelter as a boy hoping the Germans would drop 'a fourpenny one' directly on his school.

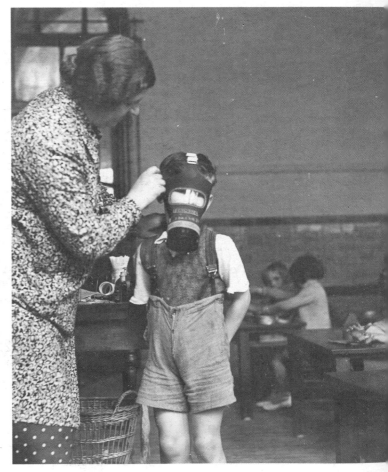

Everyone had to carry their gasmasks with them at all times in cardboard boxes. On the right is a 'Mickey Mouse' mask for small children. It was made from red rubber to make it look friendly so that wearing it would seem a game.

WARNING

If you find an old gas mask, don't try it on. Gas masks contain chemicals and asbestos which take out poisons from the air. The chemicals and asbestos break down and become very dangerous. All the gas masks shown in this book have been cleaned and made safe.

Children sometimes put on their gasmasks in class to get used to wearing them. They were not very pleasant to wear because they smelt bad, were sweaty and the windows fogged up. But at the museum the children quickly discovered that they could make a very rude noise by breathing out hard to make the sides of the mask vibrate.

Everybody was expected to do something for the war effort. Responsible older pupils operated the school air raid siren. They worked in teams of two for a shift of three hours. They had to learn the special telephone signals that warned of an approaching raid. Most school playing fields were dug up for vegetable plots and pupils took turns digging and weeding. The children thought that, although this sounded hard work, pupils in the war probably thought it was a welcome relief from schoolwork.

In spite of pupils' secret hopes, air raids did not necessarily mean the end of lessons. These children in a Bermondsey school are continuing their class in the dining room of a surburban house.

Evacuation

Cities were the main targets for bombs, so the government decided to move city children to safer areas in the countryside. About 1½ million children were sent away. This was called evacuation.

For some children, a train journey was a great novelty and evacuation was an exciting adventure. For other children evacuation was a miserable experience.

The first children were evacuated in 1939 when whole schools were moved together. Children wore identity labels, and carried their gasmasks and a small suitcase. 'We left home early in the morning with our gasmasks hanging round our necks. It was very dark. We got to the school and all the mothers. . . were trying not to cry. . . We didn't really know what was happening to us. . .' remembers one evacuee.

These children are trying to imagine how it felt to be evacuated. They decided that leaving home to live with strangers must have been very frightening. They could understand why some evacuees took a favourite toy for comfort.

In those days, children were not used to travelling long distances. By the end of their journeys, they were tired and dirty. They had to wait in a village hall to be chosen by local families. Well-dressed, tidy children were picked first. Scruffy, ill-dressed children were usually left till last. Brothers and sisters often had to be split up.

Country life was strange to inner city children, many of whom had never seen a field before, let alone a cow. Local families were shocked by some evacuees' rough city manners and swearing. Many children were homesick. Others loved the country and stayed in touch with their host families for the rest of their lives.

Some city children settled into country life very well. These people are enjoying a reunion in a Norfolk village 50 years after they were evacuated there in 1939.

The war effort

Although the Blitz caused many deaths and a huge amount of damage, no-one thought of giving up. Everyone was involved in the war effort in one way or another and every job was made to seem important. It was called 'doing your bit'.

After the men had been called up to fight, women were also conscripted. They joined the women's branches of the armed services, or became nurses or land girls helping on farms. Everyone who could work had a job, sometimes two. Married women and teenage girls worked shifts in the factories making aeroplanes, ammunition, and bombs. Teenage boys became cadets or coal miners. Grandpas watched for fires during air raids. Grandmas ran street canteens.

Those who were too frail or too old to fight, or had an important job which kept them out of the armed forces, joined the Home Guard sometimes called 'Dad's Army'. They guarded buildings, patrolled the streets and operated anti-aircraft guns.

The children had a brew-up of the favourite wartime drink – tea. Tea was served up in any crisis during the war. Mobile canteens were set up in the streets to provide hot drinks for fire crews, rescue workers and victims of air raids.

This boy is in the BBC listening post at the Britain at War Experience tuning in to a wartime recording of Adolf Hitler. One essential part of the war effort was gathering information by listening to radio broadcasts like this from across the world.

The children noticed that recycling seemed to be very important in the war. They thought that this was probably because of all the shortages. From 1940 onwards collecting salvage became compulsory. People placed their waste paper, jars and bottles, rags and bones for recycling in the dustbins which stood at every street corner. Iron railings were removed from parks and gardens to turn into aeroplane parts.

▲

Schoolchildren took collecting salvage very seriously. The salvaged metal was used to build new planes. These boys are collecting aluminium to build a Spitfire. One mother reported that her children were so enthusiastic about collecting that they took away every saucepan she had.

◀ Everything was recycled, even kitchen waste like potato peelings which were boiled up and used to feed pigs.

Rations

*Those who have the will to win
Cook potatoes in their skin.*

Radio jingles like this were part of a huge government campaign to encourage everyone to make the most of limited food supplies. Every magazine and newspaper gave 'food facts' to make people aware that shortages of food need not lead to bad health.

Before the war two-thirds of Britain's food came from abroad but as supply ships came under attack from German submarines, there were shortages. From 1940, the Food Ministry introduced rationing. Each person had a ration book of coupons for different sorts of food and had to register with a particular shop. They could buy only as much as their coupons allowed. This made sure that everyone got their fair share.

The government brought out cookery books to help people make the most of unappetising foods like turnips. These children tried out wartime recipes. They made buns with grated carrot and dried egg powder. They liked them but didn't ask for more!

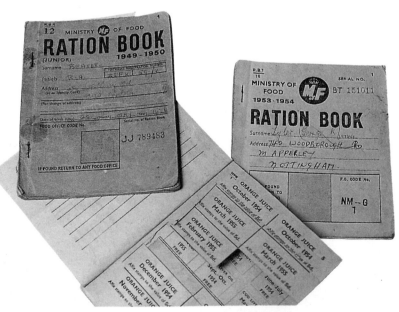

Ration books. People paid for food in the usual way but they had to produce enough coupons as well. People swapped their unused or unwanted coupons for other coupons or extra food.

1/2lb (half a pound) of sugar

3 pints of milk

3oz lard

3oz butter

2oz tea

1 egg

3oz cheese

3oz margarine

2oz (ounces) of jam

a shilling's (5p) worth of fresh meat

2 slices of corned beef

4 slices of bacon

Butter, bacon and sugar were rationed first, followed soon after by meat, tea, cheese, eggs and jam. Bread, fish, vegetables and fruit were not rationed but were still hard to find. Long queues formed outside shops which had goods to sell. One good standby was Spam (short for spiced ham) which came in tins from America. Dried egg was also useful, but whale meat never really caught on. One surprising result of wartime rationing was that the overall health of the population improved. The children thought this might have been because people ate more vegetables, and less meat and sweet food during the war years.

Here is a typical week's ration for an adult. Young children were allowed extra milk, cod liver oil and orange juice.

This boy is looking in a wartime newsagents. Most shop windows were very drab during the war. Paper was in short supply so children's comics were scarce. They were handed round until they practically fell to pieces.

▼

Making do

Everybody had to get used to shortages in the war. Many factories stopped making ordinary goods and switched to making things for the war. All sorts of things like furniture, toys, saucepans, sheets and towels became hard to buy. People patched up, mended and handed things down.

New clothes were particularly scarce and in 1941 they were put 'on the ration'. Each person had a ration book with 66 coupons for the year. A new coat might cost 15 coupons as well as its value in money. To help overcome the worst shortages, the Utility Scheme was set up in 1941 to produce a range of useful items at low cost. Utility goods, which were marked with a special sign, were well-designed but plain, and there was little choice of style or colour. Most people stuck to the rules and endured rationing cheerfully, but some broke the law by buying illegal or stolen goods. This was called buying from the 'black market'.

'Make do and mend' was a wartime motto. No one could afford to throw anything away. This boy tried darning a hole in a stocking. He is using a wooden darning mushroom to make the job easier.

The Utility mark

A clothing coupon book

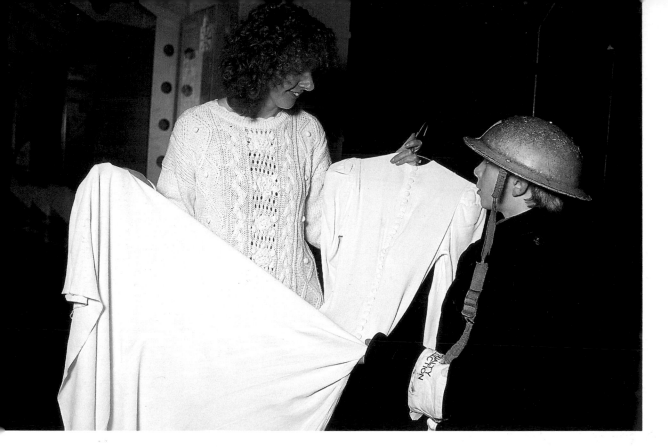

The only cloth not rationed during the war was blackout material. Unfortunately it was useless for a wedding! One of the staff at the Britain at War Experience showed the children a wartime wedding dress made of silk material normally used to make parachutes.

Wartime wedding cakes were impossible to make because of food rationing. Cardboard cakes like this were hired instead. There was a small drawer for one slice of real cake.

American soldiers first made their appearance in London in 1942 following US entry into the war in 1941. They were called GIs after the Government Issue stamp on their equipment. GIs were popular because they had all sorts of luxury goods such as chocolate and nylon stockings that had almost disappeared in Britain. Small boys followed GIs round asking 'Got any gum, chum?'

Fun and games

In spite of bombs and shortages, there was still time for fun in wartime London. Even in the shelters people played ludo and cards or had parties and sing-songs.

The cinema was very popular. Most people went to the 'flicks' at least once a week. As well as the main feature film, there was a short news film called a newsreel, and a cartoon. Famous films of the time include Disney's 'Snow White and the Seven Dwarfs', Laurence Olivier's 'Henry V', and 'The Wizard of Oz'.

The greatest home entertainment was the radio or wireless. Nearly every household had one. Some of them were old-fashioned crystal sets with earphones. Everyone enjoyed tuning in to 'Workers' Playtime' and 'Music While You Work'. The best-loved comedy programme was ITMA which stood for 'It's That Man Again'. Everyone knew the catch phrase 'Can I do you now, Sir?' which was said every week by the cleaning lady Mrs Mopp.

New toys were in short supply. Those that could be bought usually had a military theme: lead soldiers, tanks and dolls in uniforms. Most children had to be content with old toys patched up and re-painted. If anyone complained, the answer was always the same; 'Don't you know there's a war on?'

Playing parlour games was a popular amusement in the evenings. This is a special wartime version of Happy Families which shows famous wartime characters.

Collecting cigarette cards was a popular wartime hobby. This card is part of a set which showed how to deal with emergencies at home during an air raid.

WILLS'S CIGARETTES

INCENDIARY BOMB COOLING DOWN

To celebrate the end of the war, people all over the country held street parties. This one is in a heavily bombed area of south east London. People who lived there called it 'Bomb Alley'. Hanging up you can see a dummy made to look like the chief of the German air force. The tables are made from old Morrison shelters.

How to find out more

Visits

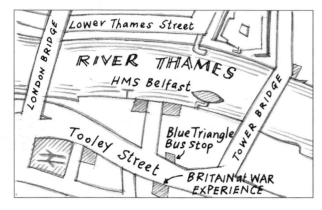

You can visit the Winston Churchill's Britain at War Experience which features in this book at Churchill House, 64-66 Tooley Street, London SE1. Tel: 0171 403 3171. The Education Officer can arrange trying-on sessions of wartime clothing, tin hats, gas masks etc.

Many of the objects in the book were supplied by Mrs Tanner's Tangible History, a hands-on history experience for educational groups in the Nottingham area. Tel: 01159 812039.

There are many museums throughout the country which feature World War II material. The Imperial War Museum, London SE1, illustrates every aspect of the war and also has special exhibitions and a 'Blitz Experience'. Tel: 0171 735 8922. The Cabinet War Rooms, London SW1, is the secret underground headquarters of the wartime British government. Tel: 0171 930 6961.

Eden Camp, Malton, North Yorkshire is a theme museum devoted to reconstructed scenes of civilian life in World War II. Tel: 01653 697777.

Things to do

Here are some ideas of things to do to help you discover more about life on the Home Front: Try some wartime cookery. Here are two recipes for unusual dishes.

Potato Pudding

You will need 340g hot mashed potato, 113g margarine, 57g sugar, 85g sultanas, pinch of salt, flour to bind, nutmeg. Sprinkle a little flour on the potatoes to bind them. Mix in the margarine. Add the sultanas, salt and nutmeg. Add extra flour to make a stiff dough. Put the mixture in a greased oven tin and bake in a slow oven until crisp and brown. Serve with custard.

Dockleaf Pudding

With the help of an adult, boil up a pan full of young dock leaves with chopped spring onions. (Make sure the adult helps you identify the dock leaves). Add a handful of oatmeal, a beaten egg and a knob of butter. Simmer for half an hour.

Make a haybox oven

The hay box was a wartime method of saving fuel. It kept the heat in a hot dish so that it would carry on cooking after it had been taken out of the oven. It worked well with casseroles.

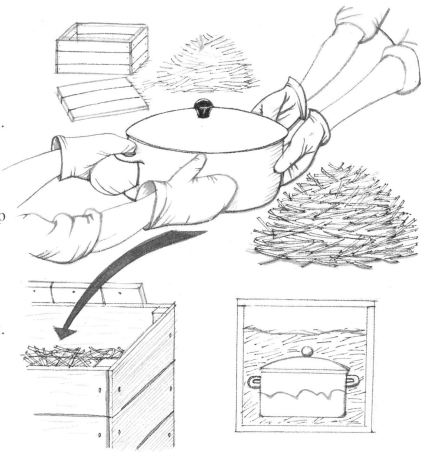

You will need a sturdy wooden box and some clean, dry hay. Pack the hay 8 centimetres deep into the box. With the help of an adult bring the prepared food to the boil on an ordinary stove. While it is still bubbling, fix the pan lid firmly in place and put the dish in the hay box. Pack hay tightly all around the pan and above it to a depth of 8 centimetres. Put on the lid of the box. The hay box should slow-cook the meal over a period of 10-20 hours.

Make a family photo album

Most families have a selection of old photos taken during the war. Ask around your relations, especially the older ones. When you have found some, mount them in an album. Write in some of your family's memories of the war.

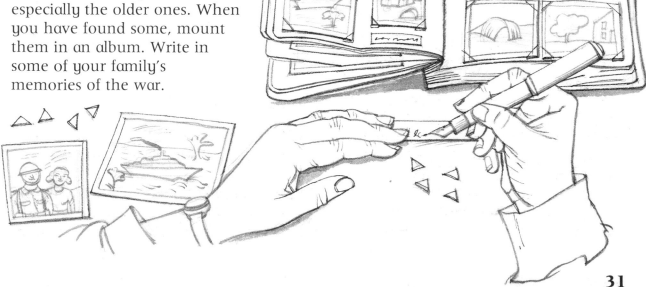

Index

First published 1996
A & C Black (Publishers) Limited
35 Bedford Row
London WC1R 4JH

ISBN 0-7136-4172-X

© 1996 A & C Black (Publishers) Limited

A CIP catalogue record for this book is available from the British Library

The author and publishers would like to thank the staff at the Winston Churchill Britain at War Experience for their wholehearted support and help, especially Allison Toomey, Education Officer, and Harvey Walker, Assistant; Gill Tanner of Mrs Tanner's Tangible History; Judy Edgar of Brewhouse Yard Museum, Nottingham; Robert Cox of the Industrial Museum, Nottingham; Jamie Bolton-Debbage, Gareth Davies, Laura Armitage, Keith Currie, Vijay Singh, Sabrina Richardson, Amar Sharma and Nareesha McCaffrey. Thanks to wartime survivors Blanche Overend, Wilfred Mallett, Ethel Powell and Mary Davies.

All photographs by Maggie Murray except: p3(bottom) Popperfoto; pp4/5 (top) Daily Mirror; pp4/5 (bottom) Hulton Deutsch; p5(right) Stanton Marcus; p8 Hulton Deutsch; p9 Imperial War Museum; p11 Public Record Office; p12 (bottom) reproduced by permission of Punch; p13(top), p16(both) Hulton Deutsch; p17(bottom) Public Record Office; p18(bottom), p19 Hulton Deutsch; p20(top) Imperial War Museum; p21 (bottom) reproduced by permission of Wilfred Mallett; p23(both) Imperial War Museum; p29(bottom) reproduced by permission of Mary Davies.

Apart from any fair dealing for the purposes of research of private study, or criticism or review, as permitted under the Copyright Designs and Patents Act, 1988, this publication may be reproduced, stored or transmitted, in any form, or by any means, only with the prior permission in writing of the publishers, or, in the case of reprographic reproduction in accordance with the terms of licences issued by the Copyright Licensing Agency. Inquiries concerning reproduction outside those terms should be sent to the publishers at the above named address.

Typeset in Meriden 14/17pt by Rowland Photosetting Ltd, Bury St Edmunds, Suffolk.

Printed and bound by Partenaires Fabrication, Malesherbes, France.